Women of Spirit Reflection Book

"Twinkle" Marie Porter-Manning

Matrika Press

Women of Spirit Reflection Book
Copyright © "Twinkle" Marie Porter-Manning
December 2022

All Rights Reserved
including the right of reproduction,
copying, or storage in any form
or means, including electronic,
In Whole or Part,
without prior written
permission of the author.

ISBN: 978-1-946088-46-8

1. Journal 2. Self Care 3. Self-Exploration
4. Spirituality 5. Philosophy 6. Keepsake 7. Title

Cover Image - Intuitive Abstract Painting by Twinkle:
"Flowers Painted at the River Studio"

Matrika Press

Matrika Press
P.O. Box 115
Rockwood, Maine 04478
Editor@MatrikaPress.com

www.MatrikaPress.com

Dedication

**To: *the Authors & Artists*
*of the Women of Spirit Book Series.***
Your wisdom and expertise has helped
countless women and girls around the globe.

To: the Women's Wisdom Groups,
*the sisterhood you offer to those in your community
is a sacred service beyond measure.*

Introduction

Reflection & Blessing Books are created by "Twinkle" Marie Porter-Manning and are a source of intentional inspiration to be used to record personal messages to the owner of the Blessing Book. These mementos and keepsakes can be used in rituals, celebrations and communions as well as for self-reflection and documentation of one's innermost thoughts, feelings and beliefs. At the heart of *Reflection & Blessing Books* is the desire to share sentiments, messages and stories that we can draw upon as sources of comfort and a reminder that we are loved. This Reflection Book was created for self-exploration and contemplation.

How to Use this Reflection Book:
This book is designed to be used as a self-led retreat that you guide yourself on. You can do it over a period of days or weeks, or complete over a weekend. Simply select a word or phrase that is meaningful to you. Place the word or phrase at the top of selected page. Use the content space provided to describe its significance. The space is kept intentionally small so as to encourage ease of this daily writing. There are daily prompts to serve as guides. Writers can spin off of these prompts or take their daily entry in an entirely different direction.

This Reflection Book is about YOU. It can be used in times of joy or in times of sorrow. It can be used to mark a milestone such as a significant birthday or important season of your life. It can be used to help you cope with a loss or transition in your life. It can be the place you affirm what is *next* for you as you cross a threshold and visualize your greatest intention for your life. It can be a book of prayers and poems you create.

The *Women of Spirit Reflection Book* can serve as a touchstone as you process an event or life cycle. It can become a treasure to be placed in your family's library as a book filled with your own reflections, beliefs, hopes and dreams you wish to pass on to your family and other loved ones.

Wherever you are on your journey, may this Reflection Book serve you well.

For more resources and rituals to accompany this book, including Blessing Stones, visit: **MatrikaPress.com/Blessing-Books**

This Reflection Book belongs to:

_____

Occasion:

_____

Date:

_____

Women of Spirit Reflection Book
Table of Contents

1. _____
2. _____
3. _____
4. _____
5. _____
6. _____
7. _____
8. _____
9. _____
10. _____
11. _____
12. _____
13. _____

14. _____
15. _____
16. _____
17. _____
18. _____
19. _____
20. _____
21. _____
22. _____
23. _____
24. _____
25. _____
26. _____
27. _____
28. _____
29. _____
30. _____

Reflections
Thoughts for Contemplation by the Author

About the Publisher
About the Author
Women of Spirit Series
Other Works by this Author
Resources

"One of the most astonishing, rare, and precious gifts
one can receive in a lifetime is arriving at
an unavoidable juncture where
everything falls utterly apart."

— Anna Huckabee Tull

What juncture was this for you?

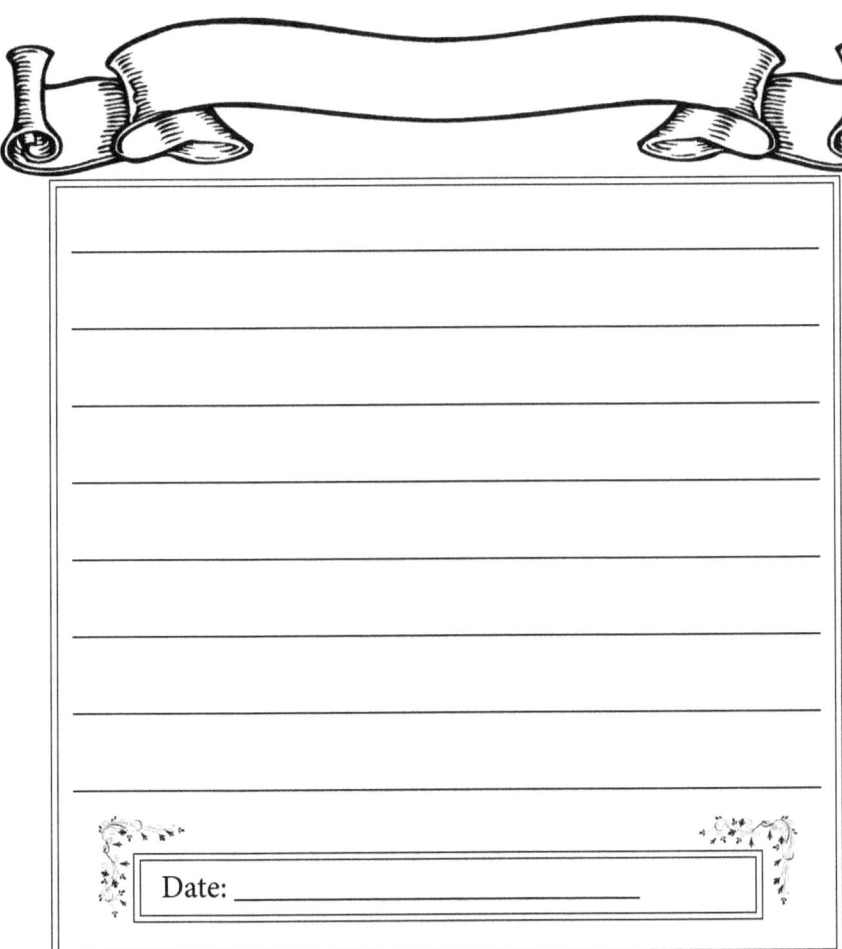

"On our planet Earth currently, we are seeing
so many imperfect manifestations and so much
human suffering because the higher bodies
of humankind have been polluted by
a flawed sense of identity, thoughts,
and impure emotions."

◻ Arica Walters

Which negative emotions and identities
are causing pain in your life?

*"In the midst of the shadows,
In a darkness that haunted,
She stood there."*

— *"Twinkle" Marie Manning*

*"I walk in the valley of fear
where darkness rules
and the air is hard to breathe."*

— *Shamananca*

What darkness has held you hostage?

*"All through the path of life,
you choose your own path,
good morals and beliefs & love gives you
direction where one's heart knows the true direction
and you yourself is its guide."*

☐ Bernadette Gahdele Rombough

What is the true direction your heart is telling you
is yours to take?

"I found myself wavering for a second time that night. How could I say no when my sons were excited about participating? How could I say yes when it all seemed so impossible?"

— Kate Early

What double-binds are you faced with at present?

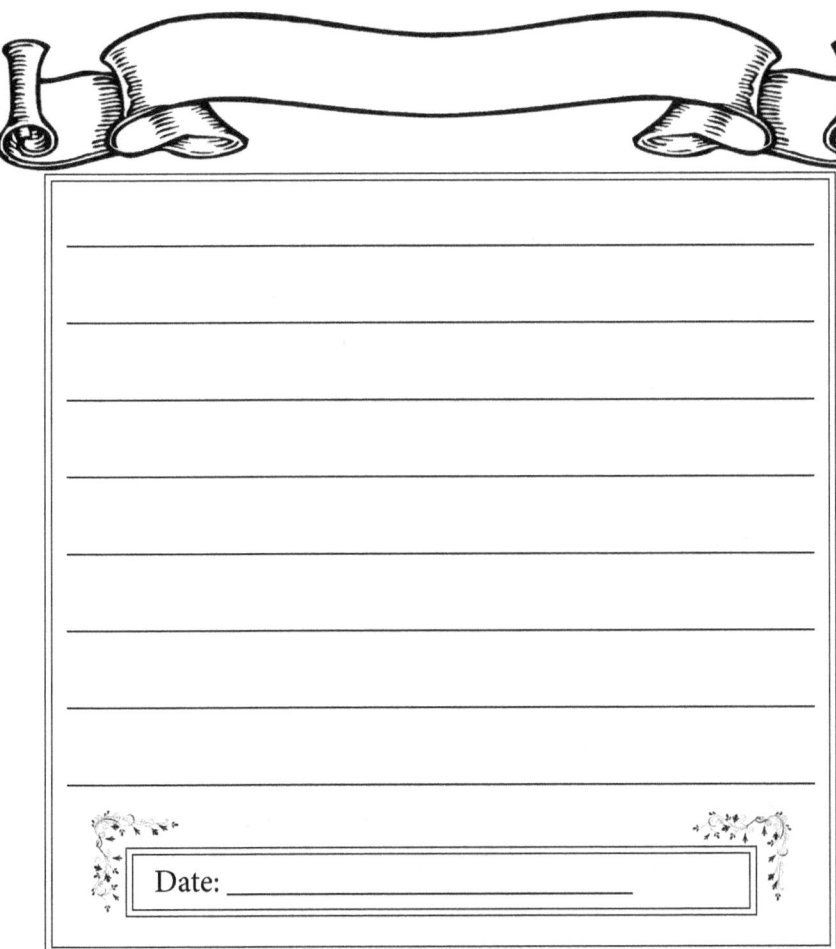

"Boundaries go both ways— around what we are letting in, and what we are giving out. Boundaries is also about leaning on our trusted people when we need to and accepting the love and support from our pillars of strength— whatever or whomever they may be. Boundaries are about giving and receiving."

☐ Erin Colene

What healthy boundaries do you have?
What boundaries do you wish to?
Who do you give and receive love and support from?

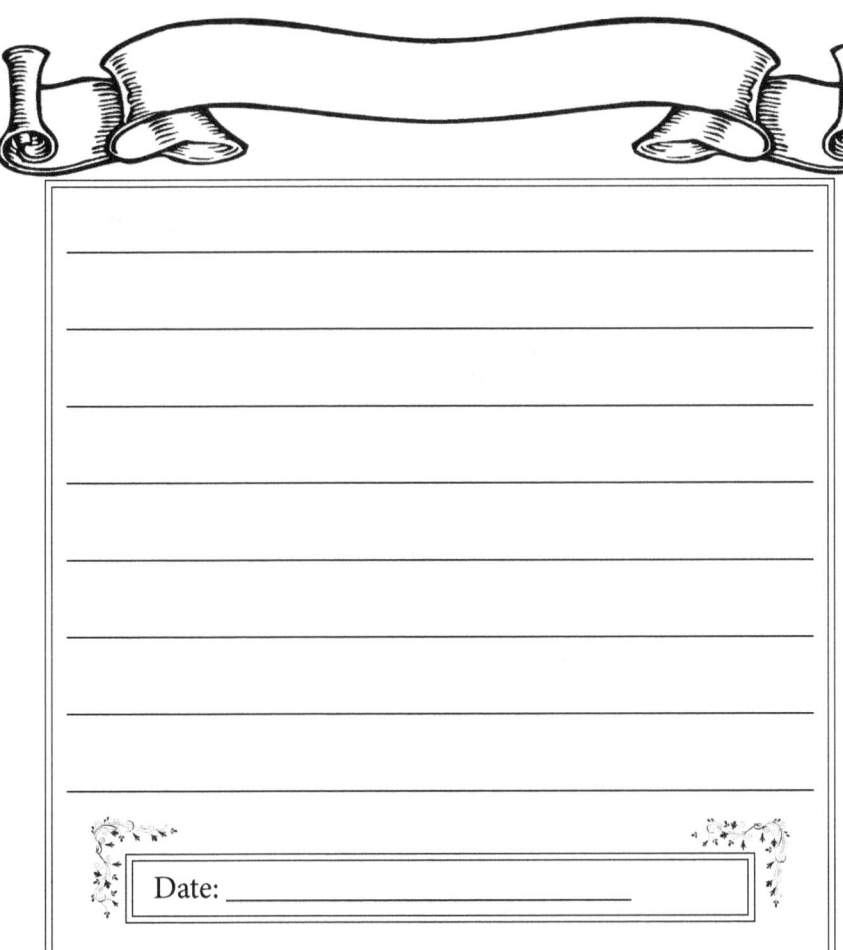

"How can I keep my faith during unsettling times? To be real with yourself and develop understanding is key; first creating self understanding and then self- healing and growth."

― Danielle Dufour

What do you wish people understood about you?

"For a lot of people, their physical reality is all that exists. Anything outside of what can be perceived using the five senses (sight, touch, taste, smell, and sound) doesn't hold truth."

— Deana Sanderson

What do your senses tell you is real and true?
What is the purpose of life?

"Who amongst us doesn't aspire to be healed physically, emotionally or spiritually?"

— Fatima Al-Sayed

What healing do you wish to have occur in your life?

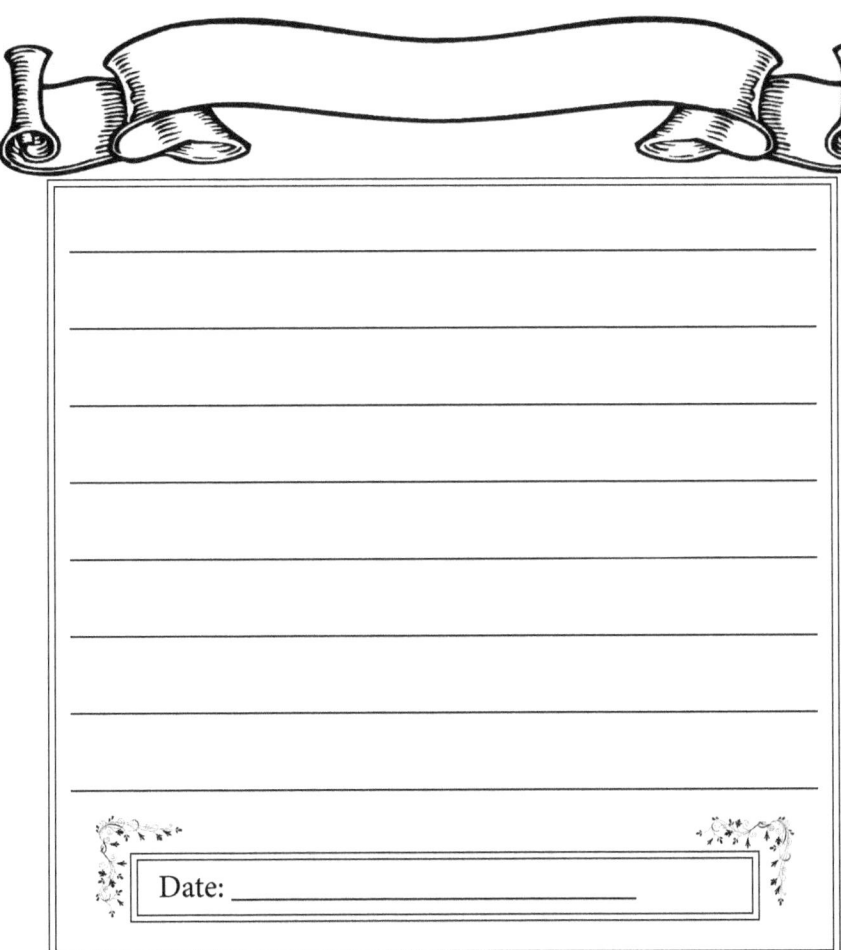

"We commonly think what ails us is outside of us, when really it starts inside the body and the mind."

— *Sloane Reali*

What is your greatest stumbling block?

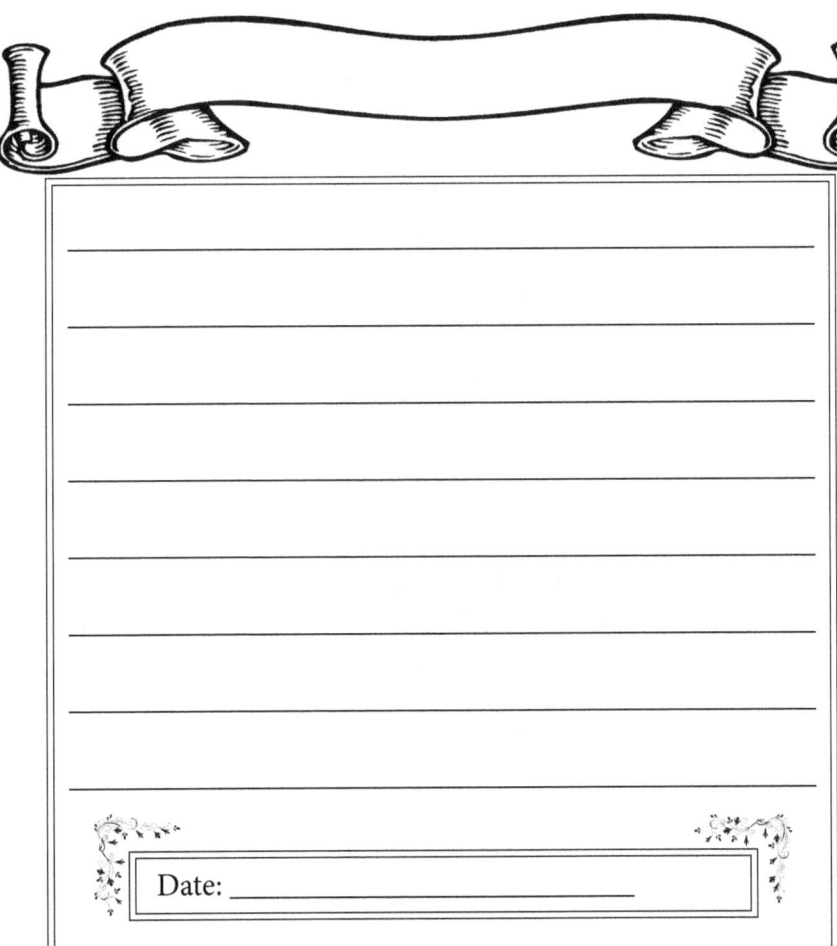

Wild Woman says:
"This breath is the wave you've been waiting for.
Freedom is here.
Power is here.
I am here in your breath."

— Kiana Love, Be Wild Woman

Many spiritual traditions encourage practitioners to follow their breath. *Close your eyes for a moment. Take a deep breath in and then a long breath out. Were you present for your breath? What thought is most present with you?*

"During healings, I felt like a bird, flying over vast expanses."
☐ Jane Sloven

"I was carried by an angel. There is no doubt in my mind."

☐ Kris Oster, Ph.D

Have you experienced the Mystical?
Describe it.

"I began to rely on my intuition and connection to Source."

— *Anya Searle*

How often do you act on your intuition?

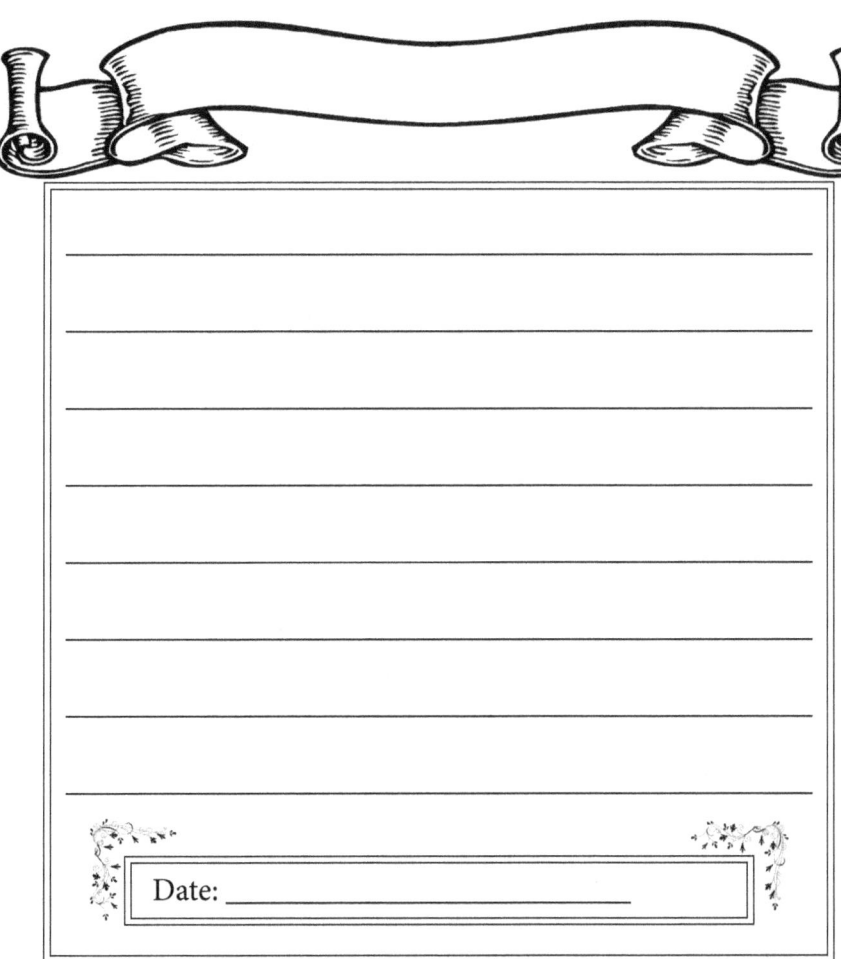

Date: _____

*"I wake up feeling very thankful most days.
It wasn't always that way.
There are times of struggle and loss
in all of our lives.
These are the times when we build spiritual muscle."*

~ Shawna Allard

What are you most thankful for?
How does focusing on that transform your mood,
your day, your life?

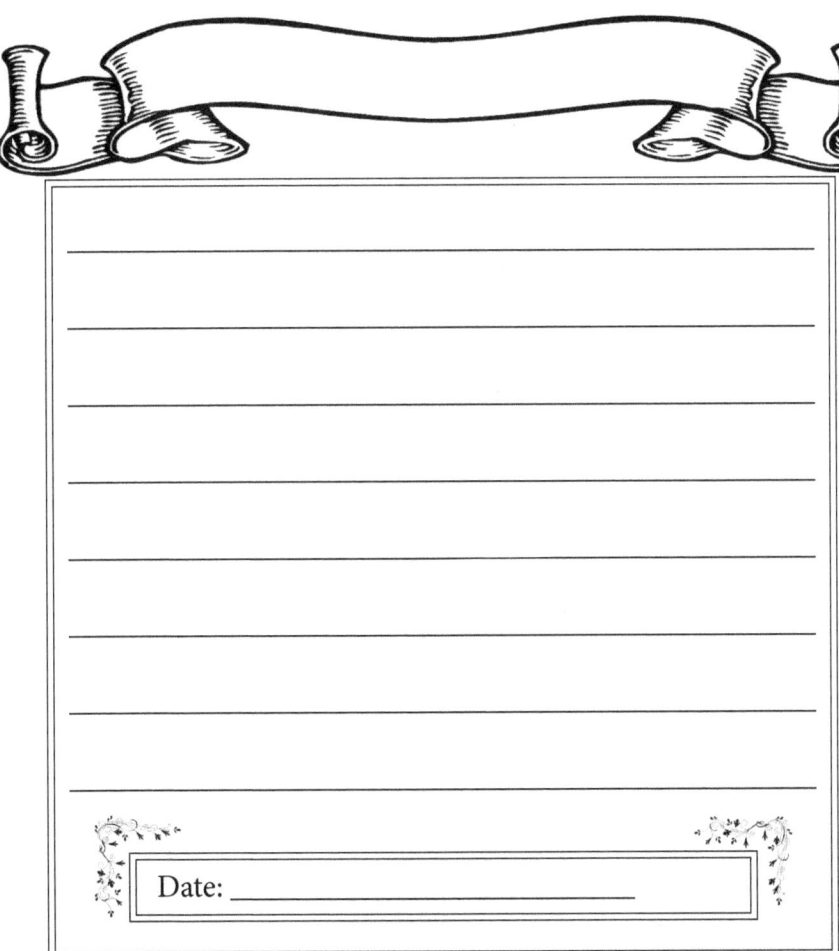

Date: _____

"My ideas are worth exploring
and my creative acts are sacred,
worthwhile and valuable."

— Shiloh Sophia

What unique knowledge, expertise and skills
do you carry with you?

Date: _____

*"I am here to offer all the wisdom I carry.
I may not even know what it is.
But it is time to share it."*

— Susan Feathers, M.A.

Who do you want to share your wisdom with?
How do you envision sharing it?

"Dare to dream of playing bigger and going for your heart's desire."

— *Meghan Gilroy*

What is the greatest vision you have for your life?

Date: _____

*"There are powerful mysteries and wonders
of life unfolding and illuminating
in you and through you."*

—*Tory Londergan*

What truths are informed by your spirituality?

*"No matter where we are headed,
we always return to the basics in life."*

*"Calm has a sound, a harmony.
It's a vibration."*

— Valerie Sorrentino

What goals do you have, and next steps
planned to take you there?
How do you access calmness even amid chaos?

"Joyous Every Day Living begins with a focus on movement, one of the basic qualifying components of being alive."

— Beth Amine

What do you do to enhance flexibility
and move your body each day?

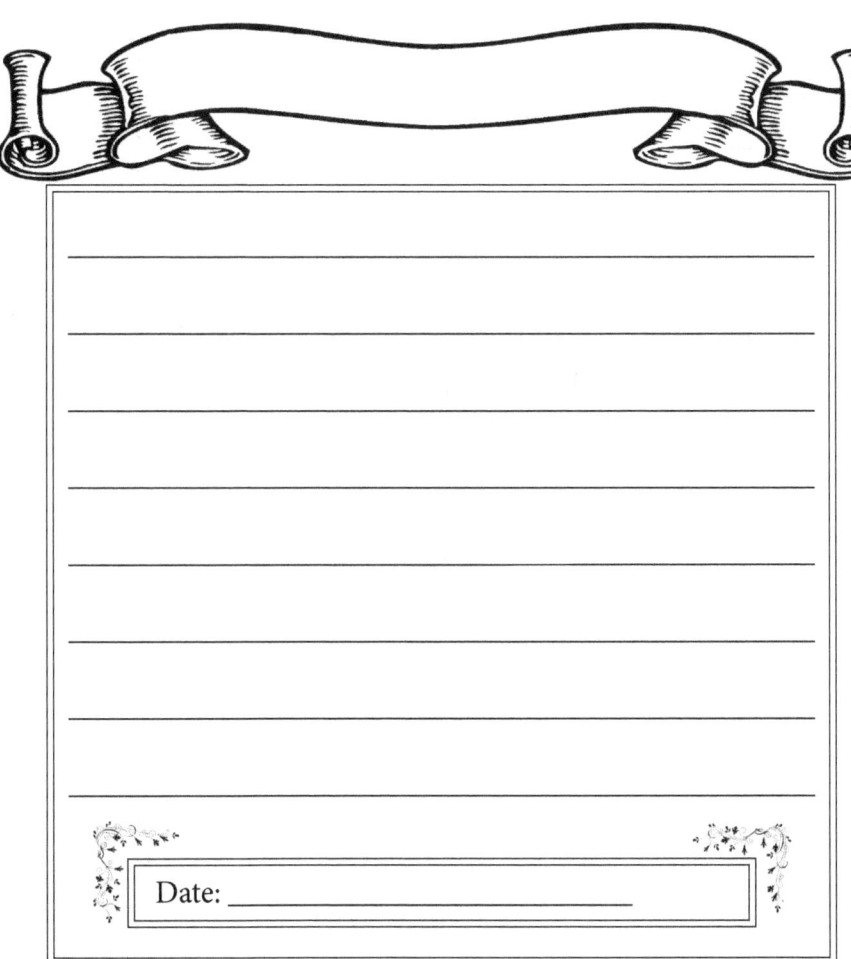

"In a world that seems to hold so much Darkness. There is always light, there is always hope."

— Melissa Kennedy

"I attempt to proceed forward in life with caution, humor, bravery, and openness."

— Jaishree Dow-Spielman

What light is in your life?
How are you the light in other's lives?

"Just as an apple seed has the potential to become
a beautiful tree that produces an abundance
of fruit or gifts to share with the world,
we are seeds ourselves at conception
with limitless potential to create and add
to the conscious collective."

— *Mika Leone*

What seeds are you planting?
What do you want to blossom more fully into?

"The purpose of the group is to give each other support and hold each other accountable for all agreed upon actions. Over time a bond develops between members, encouraging greater opportunities for growth as people come to trust the process and their fellow participants more."

— Judy Ann Foster

Whether joining a Master Mind or support group, or enrolling in a class online or in-person, we can cultivate close associates and friendships who can help us foster positivity and creativity in our lives.

What kind of group are you a part of or would you like to be a part of?

What do you gain, or hope to gain from being part of such a group?

"Every day is an opportunity to Create and Re-Create."

— Janeen Barnett

If you knew with certainty you wouldn't fail, what would you create or re-create today in your work or personal life?

Date: _____

"Responsibility is defined as the ability to respond."

— Grace Ventura

How do you respond to things?

Date: _____

*"Wins. Look at the things that went right during the month. List at least three of your favorite things that happened during the previous thirty days. Smile as you list them!
Go a step further, share your celebrations with someone who loves you.
It feels good to voice our accomplishments aloud.*

— *Tam Veilleux*

Yes, list your wins! How does that make you feel?

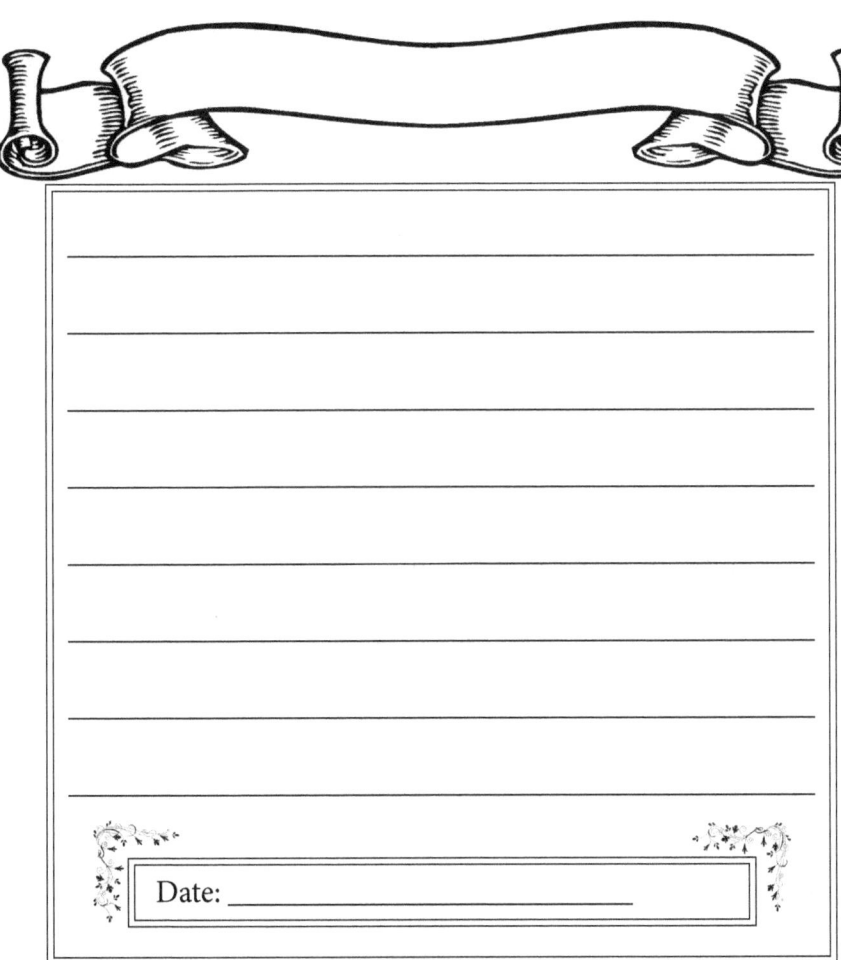

"Not perfect, but good enough."

— *Pam Swing*

We can become distracted in manifesting what we want
in our lives by holding out for perfection.
What is good enough for you?

"I've developed an ability to adapt to change and tap into a source of strength and resilience I had no idea I possessed."

"The sun, star of the show, performs its glowing entrance by reflecting across a sparkling blanket of water."

— Carole Fontaine

What is your source of strength?
How do you shine?

"You have an enormous impact with every single person you are in contact with."

— Cheryl Partridge

What do you want your legacy to be?

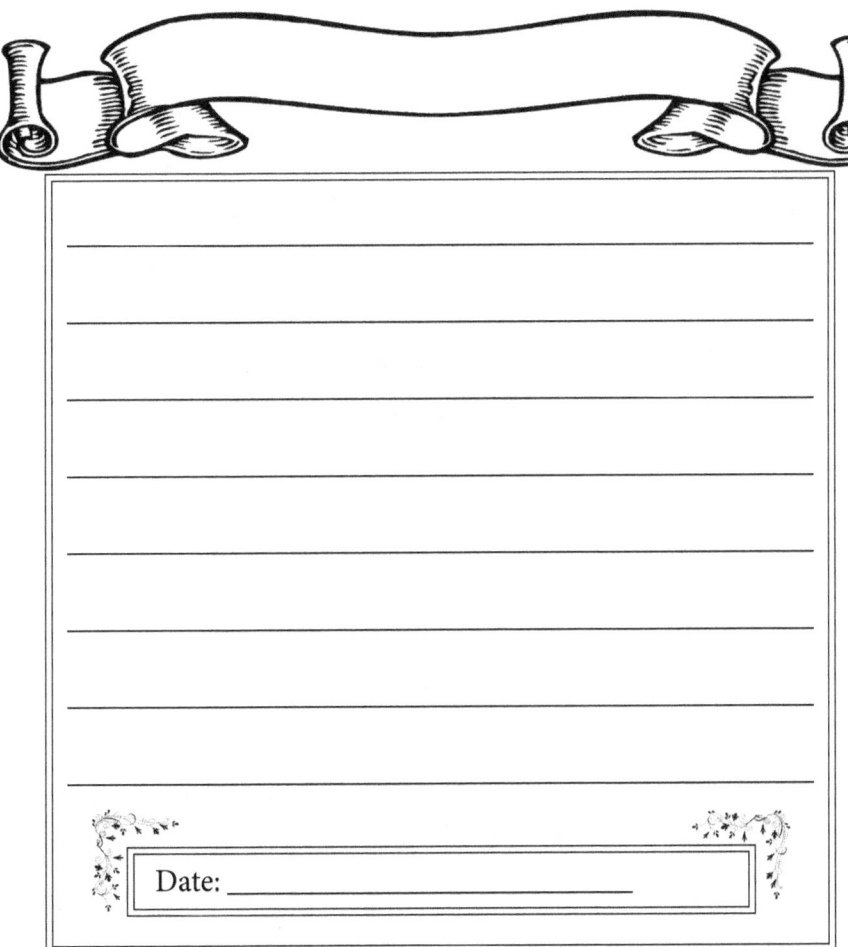

*"The manifestation of my own creativity is derived
from my awe of Nature and of the Ethereal,
in equal proportions. The motivation for creating,
be it writing or painting, often stems from
the mystery and the mysterious.
Yet, the discipline is resolutely from embodying
my physical place in the world"*

☐ *"Twinkle" Marie Manning*

What is your practice for achieving the needed discipline
to make your best dreams come true?

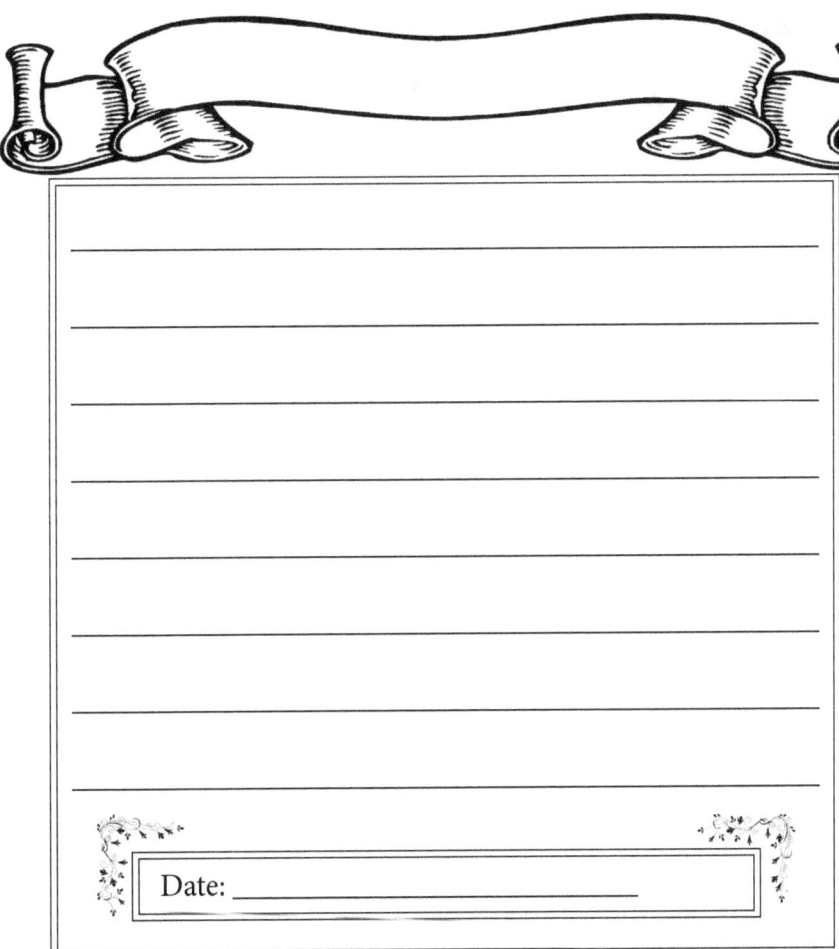

Reflections
What additional discernments have come through as you worked with the material in this book?

Thoughts for Contemplation
Including musings, poetry, meditations, teachings and prayers.

Listen
Breathe in each morning the magick of Life;
Breathe out each evening deep gratitude for living.
And Listen to the Call of the Universe
in every interaction
in every curve in the road
in every commitment to task
in every covenant of relationship
in every whispered word
in every meditation
in every prayer
in every song
Listen.

May we enter the Holy Quiet:
That place of Being that is within us,
and through us, and beyond us.

Many spiritual practices turn our attention towards the infinite, which can help us see the larger picture of Oneness, yet it can sometimes also serve as a spiritual bypassing of sorts, which can become a habitual distraction, addictive in detaching (or hiding) rather than coping with what is present in our lives.

Bringing it to the finite perspective – which is truly what we have in each given moment – is not only more manageable, but also practical in a spiritual sense because it opens the door to deep gratitude for the life we have, even if we are struggling in the moment, we are present to it and able to do something about it.

May Love be the light
and Grace be the compass
that reveal the way forward.

Consider with me this:

There is a divine echo that whispers
within every heart.
Indeed, that every soul carries with it
the echo of a intrinsic intimacy.
An original echo that is brought fourth
through time from original source.
A primal source where we are all One.
And we carry the essence of this original echo
as a talisman of our divinity.

There exists a place in our hearts where intimacy has
no limit and love has no barrier.

When one listens to the Universe,
the Universe listens back.

As a society, we treat Time as if we have
a surplus attached to a lavish line of credit
and syphon it into a plethoric gluttony
of distractions.
We are either numb to,
or feel the pressing weight of,
the tedious excess expected of our Time.
Time, a commodity
impossible to trade for its actual value.
Time, a trust fund
we cannot save for a rainy day.
Time, a gift
that comes with freedom of will.
Time, gaining equity
only in legacy.

How important it is to make every moment count.

Do you Pray?
I pray daily and throughout the day.
My life is a life of prayer.
My journey with prayer has been
an ever evolving one.
At present prayer to me is surrender and gratitude.
The first, surrender, is in communion with,
and experience of, the Holy.
The second, deep gratitude for the Holy and the
many gifts in my life. The outward appearance of
such prayers can be formal or spontaneous:
intentional moments of stillness and silence, visualization, or active with writing, creating art, chanting
or singing or drawing down the moon, walking in
the woods and along the river, speaking out loud my
heart's desires or giving a blessing, it is the lullabies
with my child each night....Prayer is even found in
doing the dishes at my kitchen sink,
and dancing in my living room.

May you live Life like a Prayer.

I believe that prayer can be as diverse as that which
we call Holy and can be made manifest through
words, thoughts and deeds, such as daily acts of grace
and gratitude.

I turn to prayer in gratitude and also in surrender
when circumstances are beyond my control. Sometimes my prayers manifest in writings and visualizations; oftentimes the simple act of touching my hand
to my heart and humming (kind of like the Om)
places me in conscious union with the divine.

My guess is, that we each have something that
we feel is Holy. And I urge you to turn to that first.
When feeling vulnerable, when feeling scared,
when feeling like you are just not quite
feeling like yourself,
Turn to that which you identify as Holy,
identify as Sacred.

When we live life as a prayer,
our reactions to situations and to people
become subtle,
even unconscious,
manifestations of the prayer
we bring in to the world.

We begin to recognize the beauty blossoming
in our own hearts and minds.
And as that beauty blossoms,
we recognize with clarity
the callings of our heart;
the *callings* from God.
And it is this,
hearing and answering our callings,
which transforms our otherwise transient lives
into union with the Divine.
This union becomes evident in the transfiguration
of our thoughts,
and our emotions.
And when this happens
we no longer need to clench when faced with
challenging situations
or difficult people.

What if hospitality
was the pillar of our Faith?

If coming together
created sanctuary?

If sharing Joys and Sorrows
was the path to enlightenment?

What if our sacred texts
were our sermons, poems and songs?

If our principles
were our doctrines?

If our covenant
was the Hope that binds us?

Indeed,
What if compassion presided
over our thoughts and our deeds?

To have resolve is to be gifted
unyielding firmness or endurance.

To practice resolve is to act
with robust commitment that is
made possible by a strong,
healthy, dynamic faith.

May it be known
That I retrieve all I am
To do all I am meant to.
From this moment on.
So mote it be.

May your life be filled with a kaleidoscope of color
and beauty and joy.

Whatever is inside of us continually flows outward;
Whatever is outside us continually flows inward.

What I am suggesting,
What I'm imploring,
And what I am asking...
...is for you to give yourself permission to rest.

Relax.
Unclench.
Breathe.

Because we belong together,
we are called to exercise compassion
towards each other,
and, towards ourselves.

It is the act of compassion that awakens us
to bring forth our best gifts to our community.

It is the act of self-compassion that emboldens us
to be brave,
and by 'be brave'
I mean it is self-compassion that allows us
to be vulnerable enough
to give over our burdens and our sorrows
into the tender loving care of our community.

Shared vulnerability,
sharing our most joyful experiences,
along with our sorrows,
this is what builds strength.

Strength in our community.
Strength in each of us.

May we build such Beloved Communities.

Beyond an altruistic "unconditional love"
is the concept of a trusted-love,
an "undoubted love."
The kind of love that is mutually intentional,
mutually experienced.
May we know how to love and be loved in return.

To attain spiritual enlightenment,
spiritual sophistication, spiritual maturity,
requires the full acceptance,
welcoming and claiming of the human experience.
This unequivocally means the integration
of our sexuality into our spirituality.
We are happier, healthier, body, mind and spirit
when we embrace and embody our sacred sexuality.
As such, the energy flowing outward from us
into our relationships and communities
reflects this well-being.

About the Publisher

Matrika Press is an independent publishing house dedicated to publishing transformational works. Matrika Press publishes anthologies, memoirs, poetry, prayer and ritual manuscripts, and other books to bring meaning and transformation to the world. A primary goal of Matrika Press is to publish stories and works that would otherwise remain untold. We also resurrect out-of-print manuscripts to ensure our historical works remain accessible.

Why the name "Matrika"?
It is said that Matrika is the intrinsic energy or sound vibration of the 50 letters of the Sanskrit alphabet called "the mothers of creation." The Goddess Kali Ma used the letters to form words, and from the words formed all things. This aligns with scriptures that assert "in the beginning was the Word," and in other sacred texts that affirm people of all backgrounds and faiths agree: Words are powerful. More than that: Their vibrations are creative forces; they bring all things into being.

Matrika Press titles are automatically made available to tens of thousands of retailers, libraries, schools, and other distribution and fulfillment partners, including Amazon, Barnes & Noble, Chapters/Indigo (Canada), and other well-known book retailers and wholesalers across North America, and in the United Kingdom, Europe, Australia and New Zealand and other Global partners.

For more information, visit:

www.MatrikaPress.com

About the Author

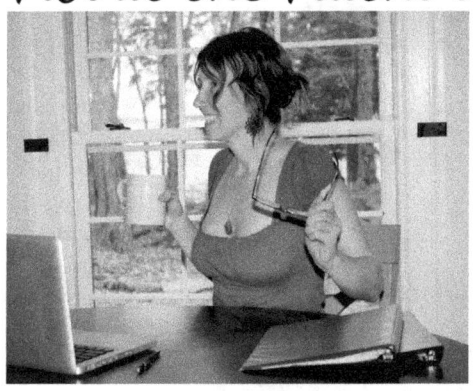

Rev. Dr. "Twinkle" Marie Porter-Manning is a semi-retired television producer, founder of *TV for Your Soul* and executive producer of the *Empowering Women* television series. She is also an interfaith minister, skilled ritualist and liturgist who has been leading workshops and seminars in the secular and spiritual worlds for more than two decades. She actively develops and leads programs that nourish spirituality. Her rituals, reflections and poetry have been included internationally in all manner of worship services and publications.

The series of *Reflection & Blessing Books* is one of her key publishing endeavors. Other published works include the *Women of Spirit* anthology series, *Intentional Visualization*, *Be Like the Trees*, *Blue Christmas*, and the *Pulpit of Peace* collection. Her debut poetry book, *Accompanied,* was published in 2021. Her seminal theology book is entitled *Living Life as a Prayer.* Her community ministry, affectionately known as *Twinkle's Place,* is located on majestic Moosehead Lake in Maine, USA. She hosts a variety of retreats and spiritual programs.

www.MatrikaPress.com/twinkle-marie-manning
www.MooseheadLakeRetreats.org
www.TwinklesPlace.org

Women of Spirit Series

www.MatrikaPress.com/women-of-spirit

Women of Spirit, Exploring Sacred Paths of Wisdom Keepers is a compilation of women sojourners, sages, mystics, witches, shaman, medicine women, ministers, philosophers, therapists, life coaches, yogis, and more.
Their journeys.
Their stories.
Their teachings and practices.
Essays, Poetry, Art, Rituals and Prayers.
This anthology is full of useful tools and powerful messages for everyone who is on a spiritual journey to embrace and enjoy. Beloved Contributors include:

- *Anna Huckabee Tull*
- *Bernadette Rombough*
- *Deb Elbaum* • *Deborah Diamond*
- *Debra Wilson Guttas* • *Grace Ventura*
- *Janeen Barnett* • *JoAnne Bassett*
- *Judy Ann Foster* • *Julie Matheson*
- *Kate Early* • *Kate Kavanagh*
- *Katherine Glass* • *Kris Oster*
- *Lea M. Hill* • *Meghan Gilroy*
- *Morwen Two Feathers* • *Rustie MacDonald*
- *Shamanaca* • *Sharon Hinckley*
- *Shawna Allard* • *Shiloh Sophia*
- *Susan Feathers* • *Tiffany Cano*
- *Tory Londergan*
- *"Twinkle" Marie Porter-Manning*
- *Tziporah Kingsbury* • *Valerie Sorrentino*

Women of Spirit, Transforming Lives is the second volume in this Matrika Press series compiled and edited by "Twinkle" Marie Manning.

Contributors include:
- *Anne B. Gass* • *Anya Searle* • *Arica Walters* • *Beth Amine*
- *Carole Fontaine* • *Cheryl Partridge* • *Danielle Dufour*
- *Deana Sanderson* • *Erin Colene* • *Fatima Al-Sayed*
- *Jaishree Dow-Spielman* • *Jane Sloven* • *Kiana Love*
- *Leana Kriel* • *Melissa Kennedy* • *Mika Leone*
- *Pam Swing* • *Patricia Diorio* • *Sloane Reali*
- *Tam Veilleux*

Feminine Callings serves as both memento and celebration of *TV for Your Soul* conversations that began in 2011 in exploration of the sacred feminine and great mysteries.

Featured guests:
ALisa Starkweather, Dale Allen, Elinor Gadon, Isadora Leidenfrost, Kiana Love, Lisa Campion, Margaret Stewart, Serpentessa, and *Starhawk.*

Hosts: *"Twinkle" Marie Manning, Lara Berry* and *Elizabeth Stahl.*

Video archives of these conversations can be found on- line, as well as are accessible on local television around the globe.

www.TVforYourSoul.org

www.MatrikaPress.com/feminine-callings

Other Works by this Author

In her seminal work, *Rev. "Twinkle" Marie Porter-Manning* shepherds readers toward realizing our intrinsic connection to each other, and to the Divine.

**Divinely inspired.
Practically written.**

Living Life as a Prayer presents a transformational theology that is accessible to everyone who wishes to embrace life in gratitude and grace. As a spiritual guidebook, *Living Life as a Prayer* outlines principles and practices to help us more deeply connect with that which we personally and uniquely identify as holy.

This book dives deep into some of the most challenging topics human beings are faced with today. Some of her themes include:

• Holy Ground • In Our Own Image
• Amalek Within • Death Changes Everything
• Envisioning a Year • Operator's Manual
• Love the Land You're With
• Let's Talk About Sex!
• Roses in Winter • Intentional Creativity
• Sacred Rebels • Mothering Mothers
• Open Hands • Sacred Service
• Hospitality - a Pillar of Faith • Undoubted Love
• Borrowed Time • Coming Home
• Love Humanity's Children With Your Whole Heart
• Fold as You Go

www.MatrikaPress.com/Living-Life-As-A-Prayer

Accompanied:
Love, Grief, Beauty, Fear, Spirituality, Mysticism, Transformation, Choices, Nature.

For the first time bound in a poetry book all their own, "Twinkle" Marie Manning's selected writings, some mystic in nature, others raw with physical-world portrayals of the landscapes we live in, created with passion, emotion, reflection and thoughtfulness.

Throughout, it is clear she recognizes our journeys are Accompanied with those who weave in and out of our lives: the people, the places, the creatures. Upon reading, one quickly realizes that, even in mundane things, the Divine is right there too.

www.MatrikaPress.com/accompanied

Pulpit of Peace:
Inspirational Quotes from a Prophetic Ministry

This book features excerpts from Rev. Dr. "Twinkle" Marie Porter-Manning's sermons, as well as glimpses of her poetry, meditations, rituals and reflections. Common themes of her ministry and writings found in this book include: *Building The Beloved Community; Möbius Life; Explorations of Divinity;* and *Living Life as a Prayer.*

Pulpit of Peace is part of the *a Pocketful Book Series*.

www.MatrikaPress.com/pulpit-of-peace

Blue Christmas:
Holding your grief sacred during this holiday season.

The holidays, while filled with light, can create palpable darkness. This *Blue Christmas* book is designed to be used as a self-led retreat to guide you during your quiet reflective moments this holiday season. It is where you can contemplate and document your inner-most thoughts, feelings and beliefs.

Blue Christmas is part of the *Reflection & Blessing Book Series*.

www.MatrikaPress.com/blue-christmas

Host a Salon Gathering, Signature Event, Fundraiser, or Concert, be a Guest, and for Sponsor inquiries, email: EmpoweringWomenTelevision@gmail.com

www.ingramcontent.com/pod-product-compliance
Lightning Source LLC
Chambersburg PA
CBHW051807100526
44592CB00016B/2598